FLOWERS BLOOM!

Mary Dodson Wade

Series Science Consultant:
Mary Poulson, Ph.D.
Associate Professor of Plant Biology
Department of Biological Sciences
Central Washington University
Ellensburg, WA

Series Literacy Consultant:
Allan A. De Fina, Ph.D.
Past President of the New Jersey Reading Association
Chairperson, Department of Literacy Education
New Jersey City University
Jersey City, NJ

CONTENTS

WORDS TO KNOW

bloom—When a plant makes a flower.

nectar (NEK tur)—The sweet juice inside a flower.

petals (PEH tuls)—The flower parts that are sometimes bright in color.

pollen (PAH lun)—A dustlike powder that helps make new plants.

PARTS OF A FLOWER

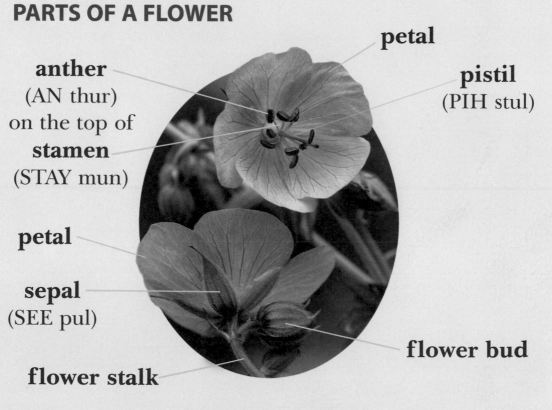

petal

anther
(AN thur)
on the top of
stamen
(STAY mun)

pistil
(PIH stul)

petal

sepal
(SEE pul)

flower bud

flower stalk

3

WHAT IS A FLOWER?

Most plants make flowers.
A flower is one part of a plant.
A flower has an important job.
It makes seeds.

dandelion flower

◄ **This cherry tree has many flowers.**

WHERE DO FLOWERS BLOOM?

Flowers **bloom** in many places. Water lilies bloom in ponds. Cactus plants bloom in the desert. Poppies bloom in cold places like Alaska. Orchids bloom in warm rain forests.

water lilies

This cactus makes red flowers.

Indonesia

Rafflesia grows in rain
forests in Indonesia
(in doh NEE zhuh).
Flies like the flower's
rotten-meat smell.

HOW **BIG** ARE FLOWERS?

Flowers can be big or small. The biggest flower in the world is rafflesia (ruh FLEE zhuh). It can be as big as a bathtub. The smallest flower is on the duckweed plant. It is much smaller than the head of a pin.

There are many duckweed plants in the water with this frog.

ARE THERE DIFFERENT KINDS OF FLOWERS?

daffodil

◄ Many flowers stand alone.

Others grow close together
at the tip of a stem. ►

bluebells

lupine (LOO pyn)

◄ Some flowers grow on top of
one another along a tall stem.

Some plants, like corn, have two
kinds of flowers.

**Pollen flowers
are at the top of
the corn plant.**

**Ear flowers below
them turn into
corn we can eat.**

grass flowers

DO ALL FLOWERS HAVE PETALS?

Some flowers have **petals** with bright colors. They might be red, yellow, or white. Birds and insects fly to the bright flowers. Grass flowers have no petals and look very plain.

petal

A white trillium (TRIHL ee um) flower blooms in the forest.

This ruby-throated hummingbird sips nectar from a geranium (jur AY nee um) flower.

WHAT IS NECTAR?

Nectar is the sweet juice inside a flower. It is food for birds and insects. A hummingbird uses its long beak to reach the nectar. Butterflies sip the nectar too. Bees use nectar to make honey.

An American painted lady butterfly finds nectar in this flower.

WHAT IS POLLEN?

Flowers make **pollen**. Pollen looks like dust. It is usually yellow, but it can be red or green too. It is made near the center of the flower.

anther
with
pollen

The anther of a flower makes pollen. (Look back at page 3 to see the parts of a flower.)

Pollen is flying off this pussy willow flower. Pollen makes some people sneeze!

HOW DO FLOWERS MAKE SEEDS?

Insects and birds crawl on some flowers. The pollen sticks to their bodies. They bring the pollen inside the flower. Once inside, the pollen helps the flower make seeds. These seeds may become a new plant someday!

This honeybee gathers pollen. It stores it on its legs.

ACTIVITY: ARE ALL FLOWERS COLORFUL?

You will need:

* a pencil
* piece of paper
* library book showing state flowers, or a computer to look up state flowers

Every state has a state flower. Find a library book with pictures of state flowers. Or look up STATE FLOWERS on the Internet with an adult.

1. What is the name of your state flower? Does it have many petals or just a few?

2. What color is the state flower of each of these states?

> **California**
>
> **Delaware**
>
> **Maine**
>
> **North Carolina**
>
> **New Jersey**
>
> **Nevada**
>
> **Ohio**

Which states do not have colorful flowers? Which states have the brightest flowers?

LEARN MORE

BOOKS

Hipp, Andrew. *Sunflowers, Inside and Out.* New York: PowerKids Press, 2004.

Loves, June. *Flowers.* Philadelphia: Chelsea Clubhouse, 2005.

Murphy, Patricia J. *Peeking at Plants with a Scientist.* Berkeley Heights, N.J.: Enslow Publishers, Inc., 2004.

Nelson, Robin. *From Flower to Honey.* Minneapolis: Lerner Publications Company, 2003.

WEB SITES

University of Illinois. *The Great Plant Escape.*
<http://www.urbanext.uiuc.edu/gpe>

U.S. Department of Agriculture. *Sci4Kids.* **"Plants."**
<http://www.ars.usda.gov/is/kids>
Click on the picture of the sunflower.

INDEX

Enslow Elementary, an imprint of Enslow Publishers, Inc.
Enslow Elementary® is a registered trademark of Enslow Publishers, Inc.

Library of Congress Cataloging-in-Publication Data

Wade, Mary Dodson.
  Flowers bloom! / by Mary Dodson Wade.
    p. cm. — (I like plants!)
  Summary: "Presents basic information about flowers, including colors, shapes, sizes, and parts"—Provided by publisher.
  Includes bibliographical references and index.
  ISBN-13: 978-0-7660-3157-9 (library ed.)
  ISBN-10: 0-7660-3157-8 (library ed.)
    1. Flowers—Juvenile literature. I. Title.
  QK653.W23 2009
  582.13—dc22   2007039462

ISBN-13: 978-0-7660-3617-8 (paperback)
ISBN-10: 0-7660-3617-0 (paperback)

Printed in the United States of America
042010 Lake Book Manufacturing, Inc., Melrose Park, IL

10 9 8 7 6 5 4 3 2

Enslow Publishers, Inc., is committed to printing our books on recycled paper. The paper in every book contains 10% to 30% post-consumer waste (PCW). The cover board on the outside of each book contains 100% PCW. Our goal is to do our part to help young people and the environment too!

Note to Parents and Teachers: The *I Like Plants!* series supports the National Science Education Standards for K–4 science. The Words to Know section introduces subject-specific vocabulary words, including pronunciation and definitions. Early readers may need help with these new words.

Photo Credits: © 1999, Artville, LLC, p. 8 (map); iStockphoto.com: © archives, p. 11 (top), © HAVET, p. 5, © Neil Scanlon, p. 19, © Sergei Sverdelov, p. 20; Photo Researchers, Inc.: Fletcher & Baylis, p. 8, Jerome Wexler, p. 17, John Mitchell, p. 7, Rod Planck, p. 9, Samuel R. Maglione, p. 10; Shutterstock, pp. 1, 4, 13, 14, 23; Visuals Unlimited: © Adam Jones, p. 10 (bottom left), © Bill Beatty, p. 18, © Brad Mogen, p. 11 (bottom), © J S Sira/Gap Photo, pp. 2, 16, © Jonathan Buckley/Gap Photo, p. 3, © Marc Epstein, p. 6, © Mark Bolton/Gap Photo, p. 10 (top left), © Nigel Cattlin, p. 12, © Ray Coleman, p. 15.

Cover Photograph: © Sergei Sverdelov/iStockphoto.com

Enslow Elementary
an imprint of
Enslow Publishers, Inc.
40 Industrial Road
Box 398
Berkeley Heights, NJ 07922
USA
http://www.enslow.com